THE HAND-CARVED CRÈCHE

OTHER BOOKS BY JAMES KILGO

Deep Enough for Ivorybills

Inheritance of Horses

Daughter of My People

THE
Hand-Carved Crèche
and
Other Christmas Memories

JAMES KILGO

HILL STREET PRESS ATHENS, GEORGIA

A
HILL
STREET
PRESS
BOOK

Copyright

© 1 9 9 9   b y

J a m e s

K i l g o .

A l l

r i g h t s

reserved.

Printed   in

United   States

of   America.

Text and cover

design by Anne

Richmond

Boston.

Published in the
United States of
America by
Hill Street Press LLC
191 East Broad Street,
Suite 209
Athens, Georgia 30601-2848 USA
7 0 6 - 6 1 3 - 7 2 0 0
www.hillstreetpress.com

Hill Street Press is committed to preserving
the written word. Every effort is made to print
books on acid-free paper with a significant
amount of post-consumer recycled content.

Library of Congress Cataloging-in-Publication Data

Kilgo, James, 1941-
    The hand-carved creche and other Christmas stories /
by James Kilgo.
        p.   cm.
    ISBN 1-892514-23-0 (alk. paper)
    I. Christmas—Southern States Fiction.
2. Christmas stories, American. I. Title
PS3561.I3668H36 1999
813'.54—dc21   99-25531
                                CIP
    ISBN # 1-892514-23-0
    10 9 8 7 6 5 4 3 2

For my mother
Caroline Lawton Kilgo,
who first taught me to tell stories,
and
for my granddaughter
Caroline Mae Kilgo,
to whom I tell them now

Contents

Preface

Letter to Caroline

My dear Caroline,

By the time you are able to read and understand these stories, the world I grew up in will have receded into history. The 1950s will seem as quaintly remote to you as the nineteenth century does to me, perhaps even more so. For the mid-twentieth century was more like my grandfather's time than your age will be like mine.

Yet through the steadily accelerating rate of change some things remain constant. I trust that Christmas is one of them. I don't mean the superficialities—the styles of decorating and celebrating—but the true meaning of the holiday. If you were to ask me what that is, I would have to answer by telling stories. The ones I'm about to tell here come from my own experience and they are true; most of them are even factual.

What I know of story telling I first learned from listening to the beautiful lady for whom you are named. Her stories were mostly about the family—her family when she was a little girl, my father's parents when she was first married, my brother and sisters and me when we were too young to remember. For her, stories were a way— maybe the best way—of reminding ourselves of who we were and what we believed; but they were always entertaining, and she took pleasure in the telling. In that spirit now I tell these tales for you. Knowing that you will someday read them gives me pleasure and makes them better than they would have been otherwise.

Love,
Papa

The Promise

The Promise

In December of 1944 the world was at war and my father had left us at home in South Carolina for Officer Candidate School in Hollywood, Florida. He sent my baby sister Caroline and me teddy bears. Mine was a panda almost as big as I was—because I was a big boy, my mother told me. He also sent me a coconut. It arrived without wrapping, stamped and addressed on the outside. My grandfather, Pop, who lived a block away from us, made a ceremony of opening it. In the spacious kitchen of his house he hacked away the hairy husk, punched out the eyes with an icepick, drained the milk into a jar, and cracked the shell. I had never tasted coconut. As he broke the moist white meat and gave me a piece, he said, "This is from your Daddy." I didn't like it but because Daddy had sent it, I said I did.

My father had been exempt from military service because of his age—thirty when the war broke out—but in the summer of 1944 he received a draft notice. With the aid of his congressman, he got an appointment to OCS, and all I had seen of him since were the photographs my mother brought home from her trip to his graduation. The uniform must have impressed her. She thought he was the most handsome man in the world, bald head and all. He had since been posted to Norfolk, Virginia. She showed me Norfolk on a map. It didn't look so far from South Carolina.

"When is he coming home?" I asked for what must have been the thousandth time.

My mother was decorating our Christmas tree. At twenty-five she had great beauty, the kind that is unaware of itself, but her dark hair and blue eyes turned heads when she walked down the aisle at church. I called her Mammy. She had long since given up on trying to explain to me why Daddy could not come home. She picked me up, handed me an ornament to place on the tree, and tried to distract me with a promise of Santa Claus.

At three and a half I was too old to be so easily put off. I had not forgotten my father, as a younger child would have, nor had I learned to abide his absence quietly. I missed him throughout the day but especially at bedtime. Every night I wanted Mammy to tell me about him, where he was and what he was doing. I asked her to read again his last letter, the part about me. Sometimes she showed me the pictures of him in his uniform. Just before lights out we said my prayers: Keep Daddy safe and make the war stop so he can come back home. Mammy promised me that God would answer my prayers, and with the faith of a child I believed.

With the same faith I believed in Santa Claus. In fact I'm sure I must in some way have associated Daddy with Santa Claus and Santa Claus with God. I could not see any of them, yet they could see me; they all wanted me to be a good boy, and they all had good things to give me. But there were moments when confusing information caused the three to separate into individuals in my mind. God was always with us, Mammy said, just invisible, and Santa Claus was definitely coming to our house in about ten days. I knew that neither of those things were true of my Daddy.

Much of what I have related I actually remember—especially the panda and the coconut—but what happened next I didn't learn until the other day when Mammy was spending the Christmas holiday with my wife Jane and me.

We were talking about the Christmases of my childhood, and she took me back to the very far side of memory, where it shades into the darkness. The next part is her story.

She had not had an easy time of it since Daddy had been away, she said. Neither her parents, who lived in Greenwood, South Carolina, nor her parents-in-law wanted her to remain alone with her two small children in the tiny house where she and my father had started their lives together. Given the choice, she found it more convenient to move in with her husband's parents. Theirs was a large house one block away, and Pop doted on me, his namesake and first grandchild. But Pop was overbearing. In all matters, from household economies to the care of young children, he knew best. Everything under his roof belonged to him, and his word was law. Mammy was intimidated by him. At night, for example, after Caroline and I were put to bed, he would have her and my grandmother, whom I called Mama, sit down and listen as he read aloud from a novel by Charles Dickens. In those days before television he thought he was providing entertainment, and he did read well, Mammy said. But she could not enjoy the story for fear that one of us would wake up at some climactic moment and start to cry. My crying he didn't seem to mind, but if the baby caused the interruption he would fuss and fume. It was not an altogether happy situation.

After a couple of weeks Mammy announced that she was taking us to Greenwood, a three-hour drive across the state which Caroline and I made in the well behind the seat of an Oldsmobile coupe. But Greenwood didn't work out either. Her father—my grandfather Doc—was bedridden with recurring migraines. Caroline had developed an ear infection and cried all the time. After a week of constant stress Mammy packed us up and drove back to Darlington, though not to Pop's big house. We settled in at home. Mammy pulled our cribs into her room, and with our Dalmatian, Buster, asleep on the floor beside her bed she felt perfectly safe.

It was in that little house that she decorated the Christmas tree; down its chimney that Santa Claus would come.

A week before Christmas Daddy called. He had been given a forty-eight hour leave for Christmas Day. Problem was, he had no way to get home. Mammy had needed to keep the Oldsmobile, and both bus and train would take too long. No matter. Mammy would somehow make it happen. In her joy she picked me up and told me that Daddy would be home for Christmas.

Then she faced the facts. His only chance was for her to drive to Norfolk on Christmas Eve and pick him up and then after a few hours turn right around and take him back. But there were problems with that too. The Oldsmobile was a two-passenger automobile. Daddy would not allow her to make the drive alone. But if she found someone to go with her, there would be no room in the car for him. The only solution was to approach Pop. He owned a Chevrolet dealership; he had cars.

Mammy summoned all her courage.

"Out of the question," Pop stormed. "John should have known better than even to propose such a fool thing."

Mammy was determined not to cry, but Pop had made her angry. "It was my idea," she said in defense of her husband, "not John's."

She waited twenty-four hours before she approached him again. He was gentler this time but no less firm. "It would take all our stamps," he said, referring to the system of gasoline rationing. "For such a short time, just a few hours on Christmas day, it's just not worth it."

"It is to me," my mother said.

"Besides, even if I had an available car, which I don't, who would you get to go with you? You can't make a trip like that by yourself."

"Why couldn't Marco go?"

Marco Wingate was a black man in his middle years who worked for Pop as a chauffeur and general servant. Pop trusted him completely and valued him greatly. But Marco had other responsibilities—a family of his own and a

8

country store to run—and with Christmas just a couple of days away he was too busy to drive to Norfolk and back. "It's just not possible, my dear," Pop said. "I'm sorry."

Mammy had no time to waste. In fear and trembling she broached the subject again the next day.

"Even if I could find a car and if Marco had the time to go—and those are big ifs—you would have to ride all the way up there in the back seat, you know."

In 1944 a black man and a white woman could not give the appearance of traveling together, not in the Carolinas, but that didn't bother Mammy. She gave her father-in-law a big hug. She knew she had won.

In the early morning of a cold, foggy Christmas Eve, Marco came driving up to Pop's house in a late model Chevy, a demonstrator owned by the dealership. The trip would take twelve to fourteen hours there and back. It would be well after dark when they got home. Mammy kissed Caroline and me goodbye at the front door, told us to be good for Mama and Pop, and promised to bring Daddy back with her.

Pop didn't like the weather. Having given his consent and provided car and driver, he was having second thoughts. The impossibility of changing his mind now had made him irritable. "You be careful now," he said to Marco, "and don't you drive too fast, you hear? I don't give a damn how long it takes."

Marco, who had long ago mastered the difficult art of getting along with Jim Kilgo, touched the bill of his chauffeur's cap and said, "Yes sir." What he did not say was that he had gotten no sleep the night before.

And here is what I remember: Mama and Pop's house—the house in which my father had grown up. With a swinging door between the dining room and pantry, a great fireplace in the front hall, a wide staircase in the back hall, and mysterious rooms upstairs, it seemed to go on forever. I could play on the floor of the large, warm kitchen, building log cabins with the red and the white corncobs that Pop brought me from his horse farm. With Pop's help I could slide down the banister of the wide staircase. Mama would set me in her lap and let me spin the globe as she pointed out to me the Pacific islands where my Uncle Bob was fighting the Japanese. On that cold Christmas Eve a fire burned all day in the great fireplace. The house was filled with the smells of good things from the kitchen, and in the corner of the front hall stood a towering Christmas tree, much taller than our little cedar, and the antique lights and ornaments seemed more beautiful.

Pop was always busy. Just because it was Christmas Eve was no reason to stop work. He bundled me up and took me with him to his office at the Chevrolet place, where he let me bang on the typewriter. From there we went to the barbershop, stopping on the way at the Post Office. As was our custom, he asked me to open the little door of his box and reach in for his mail. At Watt Brown's he set me in the booster chair himself then stood by the old black barber telling him exactly how to cut my fine blond hair. "His Daddy's coming home from the navy tonight, Watt. So make it look good."

"Oh it'll look good to his Daddy, Mr. Kilgo, even if I was to shave it clean." Watt rubbed hair tonic on his palm and held it close over my nose. "What old Santy Claus gon' bring you tonight, honey?"

"My Daddy," I said, half drunk on the fumes of the alcoholic tonic.

After the haircut came the best part, the treat I looked forward to every day—a trip to the horse farm. It was our special place, a stable and paddocks and riding rings where Pop kept and trained fine show horses, and only members of the "Jimmy Club" were admitted there. A small room at one end of the stable served as an office. It was heated by a potbellied stove in the middle of the floor. While

Pop worked at his desk, I played with a bridle, snapping and unsnapping its latch. When he was finished and ready to go, I asked if he would take me up to the loft. With me clinging tight to his neck, Pop climbed the ladder. The loft was cold and dark and dusty with hay. Still holding me in his arms, he walked from one end to the other, showing me the openings in the floor through which hay was dropped into the mangers. As we walked, horses moved below us, stamping and blowing, and the smell of horse was strong.

Back at home, we went straight to the kitchen and washed our hands and put Jergens Lotion on them. Mama gave me soup and crackers for lunch, and when I had eaten I went down for a nap.

I woke up an hour later and asked for my parents. When Mama said they weren't here yet, I tried not to cry.

Mammy and Marco had not even reached Norfolk. Marco was having trouble staying awake. When they stopped for gas, Mammy told him to stretch out on the back seat and get some sleep, she'd drive.

By mid afternoon it was raining; by five it was dark. Baby Caroline was fretful and I was whining. We wanted our parents. Pop said they would be here soon then turned on the radio for news of the war. Mama made waffles for supper.

"It's time those kids were getting back," Pop said. "I'm going to run down to the office for a while. I won't be long. If they get here while I'm gone, call me."

Mama got Caroline to bed and put me in the tub, bathing me with fragrant lavender soap. By the time I had my pajamas on, Pop was back, but he would not stop pacing up and down the hall, peering out the front door window into the gloomy darkness. Mama said, "Don't you think we'd better go on and hang the stockings and get Jimmy to bed?"

"I was hoping they would be home by now," Pop said.

The stockings were long, black cotton hose, the kind actually worn by women a generation before. Pop hung them from hooks beneath the mantle, hooks that had been there since my father was a child. Mama lifted me into her lap and read "A Visit from St. Nicholas."

The scenes evoked in my imagination by the words of the poem lay all around me. This was the house in which no creature was stirring, the bed I slept in the place of sugar plum dreams. We had no snow but at the mention of eight tiny reindeer, I gazed at reindeer figurines on the mantle, and they seemed to move with life of their own.

And when Mama read, "Down the chimney St. Nicholas came with a bound," it was into the spacious fireplace right before my eyes that he landed. That would happen sometime tonight, after I had gone to sleep. In this very hall the "jolly old elf" would go right to work, filling those very stockings, and my Daddy . . . .

When my mother related the story the other day, she said that John should have driven the car from Norfolk, allowing Marco to resume napping on the back seat, but John wanted the backseat for himself and her. So they rode through the drizzly afternoon, through Rocky Mount and Raleigh, Fayetteville and Laurinburg, down into the early darkness of South Carolina, oblivious of the passage of time. Just outside of Bennetsville, thirty miles from home, Marco drifted off to sleep. At least, that's one explanation. Marco himself denied it, insisting that the oncoming car swerved into him. In any case, they were jolted awake by a screech and crash of metal on metal, a quick, wild, bouncing ride, and a sudden, teeth-rattling halt. They were in a ditch, still right side up. John made sure that Caroline was not hurt then checked to see if Marco was all right. Retrieving a flashlight from the glove compartment, he climbed out. The other car had kept going. Marco helped John inspect the damage. The entire left side, front to back, was raked and stripped, the front left fender crumpled into the tire, apparently from impact with the ditch. The car could not be driven.

Caroline was weeping in the back seat. The whole catastrophe was her fault. She saw now how harebrained she had been in begging her father-in-law to get John home for Christmas. And it would be poor John who would catch the fury of his wrath. And maybe Marco too.

Up the road, from the direction they had come, a light was glowing dimly yellow in the mist. It looked like a store. As John started walking toward it, the headlights of a large vehicle loomed before him. It was a bus. John began to wave the flashlight. The bus rolled by, slowing to a stop right in front of Marco. "You want to ride that bus on home, Marco?" John asked.

"Yes sir, I sho' do if I can, before Mr. Jim gets here."

John thanked Marco for his help, told him not to worry, and paid the driver his fare. As the bus pulled away, John and Caroline walked through the misty dark toward the dim light of the country store, and John placed the collect call.

Mammy said it was about the hardest thing he'd ever had to do.

꽃

While I slept, Pop put on his overcoat and hat and went out into the night. Now fifty-some years later I can only imagine what he was thinking, but as a father who has been called out into the night a time or two myself, that's not hard to do. My grandfather thought he had every reason to be angry, but anger was not what he felt. His boy might have been killed, along with his beautiful daughter-in-law, who happened to be the daughter of his best friend Bob Lawton. But they were not. They were not even hurt.

As he drove north through the gloom that night, Jim Kilgo had only six months to live. Much of that time would be filled with anxiety and dread—his younger son Bob, fighting in the Pacific, lived in constant danger and so many boys had fallen; John would soon be going to sea, there were bills to pay, and in July a horse show to organize. And he had not been feeling well of late. But that night the anger that might have been, gave way before a flood of gratitude. All the way to Bennetsville he thanked God that his children were safe and coming home.

Mammy said that Pop behaved beautifully, embracing both her and John at once and holding them close. He wanted John to drive. Caroline settled in between the two men, her husband and his father, unable to keep her eyes open. Her head nodded over onto her father-in-law. She jerked it back but only for a moment. Soon sleep overcame her. With her head pillowed comfortably on his shoulder, she heard her father-in-law say, "This is a sweet little girl you have here, son."

Such was the love that was busy behind the scenes keeping the promises that made my world: the fierce determination of my young mother, the constant, nurturing warmth of my grandmother, the impulsive generosity of Pop's great flawed heart, and Marco. What moved that man to leave his family and his store on Christmas Eve and, without having slept the night before, drive a white woman four hundred miles to pick up her husband and bring him home for Christmas? I suppose that Pop offered him a bonus, but this is what I know: often in the years to come, if we were driving out the Mechanicsville Road, Daddy would stop at Marco's store and take us all inside to see him and maybe buy a little something.

Pop loved the grand gesture. On Christmas morning he lifted me from sleep, picked up my baby sister, and with a grandchild on each arm came down the wide staircase into the front hall. Imagine how we looked to Daddy. What I saw, wading toward me through the glitter and twinkle of Santa Claus, was the handsome navy officer who was my promised father.

The Lionel

The Lionel

※

Like many boys in the 1950s I received a Lionel electric train for Christmas one year—the year I was eight, I believe—but I did not take good care of it. I know men today who still have theirs, packed away in boxes or displayed on book shelves, but mine suffered rough treatment. By the following Christmas it was no longer running, and I had moved on to new enthusiasms. I remembered that train when I bought one for my son's Christmas twenty-five years ago, but since then I had seldom thought of it. Then, just the other day, when my mother was spending the holidays with us, she happened to mention it. A gift we had ordered had not arrived in time for Christmas, and she asked me if I remembered the year I got my electric train.

I said I did. I could tell that a story was coming.

John, as she always referred to my father when speaking of him to us, had gone to a local hardware store to purchase a Lionel for my Santa Claus but found that they were out of engines. They had everything else—track, transformer, and plenty of cars—but no engines. But don't worry, they told my father, the engines had been ordered and should be in any day. "Well," Mammy said, "they didn't come and they didn't come, and Christmas was almost here. We didn't know what we were going to do. We looked everywhere, all over Florence and probably Columbia too, but by that time it was so close to Christmas that everybody had sold out. And, of course, you were counting on an electric train."

She paused to take a sip of coffee. I knew I had gotten the train. I just didn't know how. And she was letting the suspense build. Finally, she made me ask what happened.

"I called the Lionel factory. The person who answered the phone wasn't much help so I insisted on talking to the president, and they actually put him on. He was very nice and promised me that we would get that engine in time for Christmas. And of course we did."

"Mammy," I said. "You really called Lionel and talked to the president?"

"I didn't know what else to do. I was determined that you were going to get that train."

"Gahlee."

How much can a man recall of the Christmas he was eight? Mammy's story opened a floodgate that had long been rusted shut. If the flow of memory brought few hard facts, it certainly awakened the senses of my childhood and it stirred my heart, where the truth is stored . . .

A scratchy recording of "Silent Night" was blaring from a loud speaker on the public square, but it was 'way too warm for Christmas. The stores around the square had propped open their front doors, and shoppers were dressed in shirt sleeves. I could have blindfolded myself at any point and told you exactly where I was by the particular aroma that hung on the still air in front of each place of business. A mingling of candy and toasted cashews meant one of two dime stores; hair tonic and shaving soap announced Watt Brown's barbershop; popcorn, the Liberty Theater, and fresh ground coffee any of several groceries. I wove my way through the crowds on the sidewalk—clumps of harried country women dragging crying children, a phalanx of black girls sporting their boyfriends' letter jackets, frail old ladies in pairs, clutching each other's arms.

Though my natural gait was a darting run, I knew better than to try it among so many people. Most of the faces I met were familiar to me; I might not have known their names, but you could bet that some at least knew mine. If I was to bump into one of those ladies, upending her with her packages, my parents would have heard about it before I got home. So I held myself to a speedy walk, anxious to get to the hardware store.

From the car last night, riding through the square, I thought I had glimpsed an electric train in the window, and I wanted to check it out. Sure enough, there it was, amidst holiday decorations, a Lionel steam engine going round and round an oval track, pulling a line of colorful cars and the neatest little caboose. I wanted a train from Santa Claus. I had put in that request weeks ago, and maybe this would be the very one.

I knew all about Santa Claus, of course. I was eight years old. I had known even last Christmas, though I had struggled to deny it. But there was no hope of denial this year. In front of the train in the window, printed on a card for any child to read, was the price: $29.95. And that created a new problem. If I no longer had to worry about whether or not I had been good enough for Santa to bring me what I wanted, I had now to wonder if Daddy could afford such an expensive gift. Twenty-nine dollars and ninety-five cents was an awful lot of money, and I had two little sisters and a brother. They still believed, but Christmas would not cost my parents any less because of their faith.

In front of the grocery store next door stood a peanut roasting machine. Through a little window you could see the peanuts turning over and over. They smelled so good that I thought I would die if I could not have a bag. But my pockets were empty, and I knew better than to go to my father's filling station and ask for a dime.

Sanders Street was two blocks long. At the western end, in front of the National Guard Armory, stood a great Darlington oak, said to be the world champion of the species. At the other end, facing the oak, was my grand-mother's house. In winter when the trees that lined the street were bare of leaves, I could sit on the roots of the oak and see clear to Mama's front door.

We lived in a small shingled house at the end of the first block, exactly halfway between the oak tree and Mama's, at the place where the pavement stopped.

There were no boys of my age living on that block, yet I had seen by the time I was six the interior of almost every house on both sides of the street. Most of the residents were elderly, none more so than Mr. Jim Kirven, a blind man with a prodigious belly and a white shingle of a moustache. He often sat on the front porch of his fine old house, basking in the afternoon sun, and if I spoke to him as I walked past, he would always call out, "Heyo son, come on up here and sit a spell."

Mr. Jim kept candy in his pocket, hard candy wrapped in cellophane, that he gave to neighborhood children, but that was not the reason I stopped to see him. I just liked to hear him talk. His accent was unlike any I had ever heard. I know now that it was an authentic relic of the nineteenth century—as a boy he had known Confederate soldiers— and it appealed to my ear. On my way home from the square I passed his house. I spoke and he summoned me.

Mr. Jim had a joggling board on his porch. In the coastal area of South Carolina, a joggling board—a wide cypress board supported by stands at either end, long enough to be limber and springy enough to bounce a child pretty high—was a means of entertainment. Every one I ever saw was painted green. When I visited Mr. Jim I sat on the joggling board.

"Mighty warm, ain't it?" he said.

"Yes sir."

"Ought not to be this warm at Christmas time. Never knew it to be."

Mr. Jim had an empty eye socket on one side and a dim unseeing eye on the other yet managed somehow to speak with a twinkle. "Yo' folks doing all right, I hope?"

"Yes sir."

"I don't reckon you remember yo' granddaddy, do you?"

"Yes sir."

"Jim Kilgo. That's yo' name too, ain't it?"

"Yes sir."

"I used to enjoy watching that man ride a horse."

I had heard that Mr. Jim had once been a horseman himself, but I could not imagine him young enough to swing into a saddle.

"We raced around the public square one time, me and him and some of them other boys. I wouldn't be a-tall surprised if he didn't win. He sho could ride a horse now. And kept some fine ones too. You remember them horses a-tall?"

I was bouncing on the joggling board. "A little bit," I said.

"He's been gone some little time now, ain't he?"

"Yes sir."

Mr. Jim dug into the pocket of his coat and retrieved a handful of candy. "You give some of this to yo' little sisters now, you hear?"

"Yes sir."

"What's ol' Santy Claus gonna bring you, son?"

I looked at his empty eye socket and his red nose spider-webbed with broken blood vessels, his stained trousers pulled up high over his round belly by a pair of red suspenders. If Santa Claus ever got that old, Mr. Jim was what he would look like.

"An electric train," I said. "A Lionel."

"Ho now," he said, "ain't that something."

The next day was Sunday and Sunday night was the Christmas pageant at our church. I was not happy about it. I had wanted to be Joseph because of the prominence of his role in the story, but Joseph's part had gone to an older boy. I had accepted that disappointment with good grace, confident at least of wise man status, which was not a bad second best. I would get to dress in bright colors and wear a crown. But I was to be denied even that modest distinction. When the parts were handed out, I was a shepherd again, as I had been last year, a leftover in a drab bathrobe.

To make matters worse, my friend Phil, a whole year younger and new to the church, was going to be a wise man. The gross injustice was almost more than I could handle. The night of the pageant, as shepherds and kings huddled in the small vestibule, Phil was gloating over his superior status.

Phil was a relative newcomer to the Sanders Street neighborhood. Two years earlier his family had moved into a house in the second block, down the unpaved hill and across the street from us. Since then we had been inseparable, but our friendship was based on competition. Because his father was a minister (though at the time without a church), Phil enjoyed a professional superiority to me in all things religious. That's why he got to be a wise man, he said.

"It is not," I said.

"Is so."

"Is not."

"Then why, smarty pants?"

"Because they needed a short little person," I said. "Lester is the big wise man and Steve is the middle size one and you're the runt."

Phil gave me a shove and I shoved him back. He fell into a smaller shepherd whose beard came untaped. The small shepherd started to cry.

Mrs. Richardson, the director of the pageant, caught me by the ear. In a harsh whisper she said, "Jimmy Kilgo, if you cause one more bit of trouble, you can just go sit in a Sunday School room until the pageant is over. Is that understood?"

"Yes ma'm."

Just then through the cracked door to the sanctuary came the voice of the narrator: "And there were in the same country shepherds abiding in the field . . ." Mrs. Richardson whispered in my ear, "This is about the birth of Christ. Now act like it!"

And with that she herded the line of shepherds into the aisle.

I pouted all the way down to the manger. At least I was getting an electric train and Phil wasn't. At least, he hadn't said he was. I visualized the Lionel in the store window, going round and round the track, puffing smoke from its smokestack, and I forgot about having to be a shepherd.

One afternoon the following week, in the brief hour between school and dark, Phil and I, along with a friend named Bobby, were playing in Phil's backyard. His family's property backed up to the wooded Swift Creek bottoms; along the edge between the yard and the woods ran an embankment, and we were digging out a machine gun nest in the soft, sandy loam. The dispute was over who would get to be the heroic American soldier defending his emplacement against the charging Germans. Phil claimed the right to be the American—it was his property, he said—but Bobby proposed that we draw straws. I drew the longest and Phil got mad. For Christmas, he said, he was getting a real machine gun, army surplus, and then he would be the American soldier any time he wanted to because his daddy was not going to let us play with it.

I told him he was lying.

"I am not," he shrieked.

"Well, you can get a bazooka for all I care," I said. "I'm getting a Lionel electric train."

"I am too," he said.

He just didn't know how to back down.

"You don't even know what a Lionel is," I said.

Phil wanted to fight, but Bobby said that Santa Claus was bringing him one too and then we'd all have electric trains.

I turned on him in astonishment. Santa Claus? Bobby was my age. I didn't know a third grader in our school who still believed in Santa Claus. Even Phil, a year behind us, had all but lost the faith. But glad to ally himself with any opponent of mine, he had suddenly become a firm believer again.

I felt betrayed, not by Phil but by Bobby, who was supposed to know better. Like Phil, he had moved recently to the neighborhood. His family lived a block away, up Sanders Street and around the corner, across St. John's from Mama's house. I spent almost as much time with him as I did with Phil, but it was not often that the three of us

31

played together. Inevitably, two would take sides against the other, as was happening now.

I challenged them to explain to me how Santa Claus could visit every house in the world in one night—he wasn't God. Phil said he almost was. I told him that was the dumbest thing I'd ever heard him say, and then he played his trump: his daddy had said so and his daddy was a preacher, and besides that I was on his property.

There was no point in trying to reason with idiots, I decided. I turned to walk away, and Phil began to chant, "Anh nanny boo boo."

I turned around and started back, my fist cocked. "If you don't shut up, pipsqueak, I'm going to bust your little butt."

My ability to back up my threat was by no means a foregone conclusion. Phil was a tough little scrapper. But this time he ignored me and invited Bobby inside for milk and cookies.

I trudged up the hill feeling very much left out. If the truth had made me wiser, it had not improved my spirits. I almost envied Bobby and Phil, but I could not pretend to believe when I did not. Except around my little sisters and brother. Knowing more than everyone else was a lonely job.

I entered our house by the back door and went straight to my room. Our record of Gene Autry's "Rudolph the Red-Nosed Reindeer" was playing in the living room, which meant that my little brother Johnny, still toddling about in footed pajamas, was standing at the console watching the turntable go round and round. He would remain rooted to the spot until somebody turned off the record player. Every day my mother had to choose between listening to "Rudolph" all afternoon or have Johnny fussing underfoot. Right now she was talking on the phone. It was almost time for Daddy to be coming in from work. My little sisters were busy in their room next door, Sister Caroline getting Maisie pumped up about Santa Claus. Sister had been having doubts herself. She had confessed them to me. Now, by stoking Maisie's excitement, she was trying to talk herself back into strong belief. I lay down on my bed in the dark, hoping that Daddy could afford the Lionel. Maybe I could pray for it. Mammy said God answered our prayers. But I couldn't see any difference between that and writing a letter to Santa Claus.

At four o'clock on Christmas Eve, Mammy and Daddy got us dressed and loaded into the car. It was time to go to Mama's. We did that every year, gathering in the spacious, well-lighted house to open presents with Uncle Bob and Aunt Sis and Daddy's sister Aunt Mae, home from

Spartanburg for the holidays. After the presents the grownups would sit down for a supper of oyster stew while the four of us ate waffles in the kitchen.

I was old enough that year to be designated "Santa Claus" in the delivering of gifts. I stood at my post beside the tree in growing exasperation. The grownups, enjoying sherry and toasted pecans in the living room, would not leave their talk or even bring it out into the hall. "Come on, y'all," we whined, "it's time to open presents."

When at last they were seated around the tree, Sister without warning launched herself into Daddy's lap, knocking his glass from his hand. It shattered on the floor and the smell of alcohol filled the room. Daddy started from his chair with a mild expletive, Sister began crying, and Aunt Mae swooped down upon the calamity with a speed and determination that were a wonder to behold. Grabbing me in the same motion, she said, "Run to the kitchen, son, and bring me a dish towel, and the broom and dust pan from the pantry." Aunt Mae could not abide disorder.

She was a brisk woman with beautiful copper-colored hair. In her mid-thirties, she no longer had any hope of finding a husband, if she'd ever had, and the family was resigning itself to her spinsterhood, as the state of unmarried older ladies was called in those days. But any sympathy for Aunt Mae was misplaced. She certainly did not feel sorry for herself. She was too busy setting the world in proper order. In Spartanburg she was Alumna Secretary for her alma mater Converse College. When she came home to Darlington a large part of her work was to protect her mother's house from the ravages of her four nieces and nephews. She loved us fiercely. As far as she knew, we were the only children she would ever have to call her own. But that did not stop her from regarding us as savages in need of civilizing. In fact, it made her more determined to render us fit for polite society, a commentary on our mother which was not altogether appreciated. Yet, among the four of us, there were always shoes to be polished, laces tied, shirts tucked in, noses wiped, necks washed, hair cut, and table manners refined. Who could doubt the love in such vigilance against disorder?

I was searching in the kitchen for a dish towel when I heard a soft rapping at the back door. I opened it and there stood Howard, my grandmother's yard man. I say man, but at the time I wasn't sure how old Howard was. He didn't strike me as a grownup, yet he seemed too old for a boy. I mean, he had whiskers, but he also had a "What-me-worry?" smile on his face that caused people to treat him as a child. Hardly taller than I, he seemed forever arrested in some middle ground between youth and adulthood. Most of the time he slept in an old, unused stable in Mama's backyard, though he had been known in warmer weather to sleep under people's houses.

Howard did yard work not only for Mama but for other elderly widows as well, riding around town on a bicycle that seemed to defy the law of gravity. He draped himself in woolen rags summer as well as winter, kept cotton stuffed in his ears, and almost always suffered from a cold. When his employer of the day offered him a midday meal, he invariably declined, requesting only a glass of warm water and some peanut butter for a sandwich. He always had his own loaf of bread and a box of Ritz crackers, which dangled from the handlebars of his bike.

I doubt that my grandfather would have put up with Howard, but since Pop's death the little man had become a part of the family landscape. He too called my grandmother "Mama."

"Tell Mama, Christmas gif'," he said, but he spoke in such a rapid, husky whisper that I had trouble understanding him.

"What?"

He repeated the request.

That peculiar greeting, as I would learn in later years, had its origin in plantation society. According to the rules of the game, the black person who said "Christmas gif'" to a white person in the big house before the white person could say it to him received a gift. The custom had been appropriated by whites and in some families had been handed down to the present generation. I thought it was terribly old-fashioned.

I was still at the door with Howard when Aunt Mae came flying into the kitchen. "What on earth, son . . . Howard? What in the world do you mean, coming up here tonight?"

"He wants Mama."

"Well, Mama's busy. Howard, you run along now. We're having our Christmas Eve."

As Mae tried to shoo Howard from the door, I returned to the party around the tree. I wanted Mama to know that Howard was on the back porch asking for her, and I didn't want anyone else to hear, but Mama was deaf and I had to speak up.

"Howard?" She stood up. "Well, I'd better see what he wants."

Mama was a gentle person. With soft white hair, a generous bosom, and a sweet expression on her face, she seemed to me the ideal grandmother. Her deafness enhanced the impression. When she failed to understand what you were saying to her, she would simply smile and nod, willing to agree with whatever you were trying to tell her. I often

37

spent weekends at her house. After supper, when the weather was pleasant, we would walk around the block to the library, and when we got back home she would read to me the books I had checked out. They usually had to do with horses or wild animals. Just before bed she would prepare baked apples and ice cream.

On the way back to the kitchen, we ran into Mae, armed with the equipment she had sent me for. She said that she had gotten rid of Howard.

"Well, I'd better see," Mama said. She knew that it would take more than Mae to run Howard off. The soul of patience, the little man would wait at the back steps until he thought it was time to try again. Mama opened the door onto the back porch and there he stood.

"Christmas gif', Mama."

How my grandmother could pick up that husky whisper when the rest of us had to raise our voices I never understood, but they seemed to have no trouble communicating.

"You're supposed to wait til Christmas morning to say Christmas gif', Howard. This is Christmas Eve. You come back in the morning and I'll have something for you."

"Christmas gif'."

"Christmas gif', yourself," Mama said.

Howard disappeared into the darkness with that smile still on his face.

I wondered where he would sleep that night. With no family and no warm bed, he would have no Christmas at all. "What are you going to give him?" I asked my grandmother.

"Howard doesn't really want anything," Mama said. "I'll find something for him in the morning."

At the age of eight I was not quite capable of imagining myself in Howard's shoes outside Mama's house, looking at the lighted windows, hearing the sounds of gaiety, and smelling perhaps the aroma of good food. But throughout the rest of the evening, as I delivered presents, I was puzzled by what Mama had said. It was clear that Howard needed a bunch of stuff. How could he not want anything? I couldn't imagine it.

The presents I received helped to relieve my anxiety about the train. From Uncle Bob and Aunt Sis I got a Boy Scout pocket knife and from Mama a billfold with a cellophane window for a photo, though I couldn't think of anyone to install there. Aunt Mae gave me some kind of educational jigsaw puzzle that I had no immediate interest in. With nothing left to open, I entertained myself by opening and closing my knife. I was certain that Howard would like to have a pocket knife, but I wasn't about to offer mine.

※

Once we had eaten supper we were anxious to leave. We still had the best part of Christmas Eve to go. It started with Daddy riding us around town to look at decorations. It was still early but the streets were mostly empty of traffic. The trees a-glow in the windows of houses we passed, warming with colors the living rooms in which they stood, gave me a cozy feeling. I was reminded of the lines from the carol "O Little Town of Bethlehem": "Yet in thy dark streets shineth the everlasting light. The hopes and fears of all the years are met in thee tonight." I had little idea of what the lines meant, but they confirmed that this, of all the nights of the year, was truly the night of nights.

Our tour of the town ended with a ride around the square—the best saved for last. The splendor never failed to excite our admiration. "Ah," we said, and little Johnny cried, "Yook at the yights."

They were strung from light pole to light pole—bulbs of red and green and blue and orange—all the way around; they ascended the city hall, outlining the stately building clear up to the clock tower. And squat in the center of the square shone the courthouse, its massive columns front and back spiraled with chains of luminous color, its dome wound round and round and round to the star that glowed at the top. It was almost enough to restore your belief in Santa Claus.

Home again, we hurried to our rooms to get ready for

bed. By the time we had our pajamas on, Daddy had started a fire and Mammy came in with a tray of hot chocolate. The stockings we hung were the same old black cotton hose we had used from the beginning, but now there were four. Sister and Maisie and Johnny were trembling with excitement, their fervent little hearts untroubled by any shadow of doubt. Santa Claus was coming tonight. Maisie was about to wet her pants. I decided to join them. It was easier to pretend than to stay out in the cold. And somehow pretending, if I could manage it, helped to take my mind off the possibility that I would not get the train.

Johnny crawled up into Daddy's lap and opened the book. The rest of us arranged ourselves at Daddy's feet. The reading was "A Visit from St. Nicholas."

In later years Daddy would read to us *A Christmas Carol*, a chapter each night, but that year the others were still too young for Dickens. I on the other hand was too old for Clement Moore. Instead of the spacious fireplace at Mama's house, which had once provided me with the image of Santa coming down the chimney, I now had to make do with the little coal grate in our small living room.

When the poem was finished, Daddy reached for the Bible. "Now it's time for the real Christmas story," he said.

Inwardly I groaned. I knew that the excitement tonight was supposed to have a lot to do with Jesus, but to hear the

Bible verses while I was trying to generate faith in Santa Claus was a terrible distraction.

And it came to pass in those days that Caesar Augustus sent out a decree . . . .

We endured the Bible story, then set out a plate of cookies and a glass of milk for Santa Claus, and piled into bed—all four of us into the girls' double bed, and Mammy tucked us in. Sister and Maisie were full of questions as to how Santa would do this or know that. Mammy told us to be quiet and lie still and listen. Usually, he didn't come until children were sound asleep, but you never could tell about Santa Claus. There was a moment of breathless silence, and then, sure enough we heard something. A scrape on the roof? Even I heard it. The obvious explanation was Daddy, but the prospect of his taking a ladder and climbing onto the roof was almost as preposterous as believing that it was a fat man in a red suit. We didn't even own a ladder. Yet I had heard something.

Mammy said our prayers, kissed us each good night, and quietly closed the door. When she was gone, we tried to lie still, but Maisie kept popping up and looking all around, as though she expected Santa Claus to come right into the bedroom. Suddenly, she squealed, jumped from the bed, and ran to the window. Trembling, she danced up and down, looked back at us, then back to the window, then back at us again. She could hardly speak. "I saw him," she gasped. "Oh I really did. I saw him right out there."

In her there was no consciousness of a need to prove to herself or to anyone else that Santa Claus was real. She had seen him. She was sorry that we had not. It was that simple. She was sharing the good news.

"What did he look like?" Sister asked.

"Like he's s'posed to," Maisie said.

We were wide awake at four in the morning. Going back to sleep was impossible, but so was getting up. Venturing into the living room without Mammy and Daddy was out of the question, and we were under strict orders not to wake them before six. The agony of waiting was intensified threefold for each of us by the impatience of the others. At ten after four I decided that our parents would have to compromise on five. It was the longest hour.

I was closer to believing that our house really had been visited in the night than I had been since Christmas morning a year ago. In fact, by the time I woke up faith had miraculously reestablished itself, and unbelief was occurring only in momentary lapses. And I found this to be true: During periods of faith, it was possible to believe that in a little while I would actually find a Lionel electric train laid out on the living room floor, for Santa Claus was not subject to the constraints that bound my parents. But when common sense asserted itself, reminding me that Santa Claus could not possibly have visited every house in the world, or even in Darlington, and that electric trains were real expensive, I fell prey again to fear.

At five on the dot I sent Sister to wake Mammy and Daddy. She came back too quickly. "Thirty more minutes," she said.

"We'll give them fifteen."

We huddled at the door in our pajamas, Mammy standing guard while Daddy went in to turn on the lights. From the living room came the soft, yellow glow of a table lamp, and Daddy said okay.

We crossed the darkened dining room, not running, almost hesitant, in fact, as though that which we had so eagerly anticipated might disappoint, or worse, might not even be there. And, behold, the glory of Santa Claus: a room full of shiny new toys. But I could not have named a single one, for everything in that room, even the Christmas tree, was outshone by the Lionel electric train in the middle of our ordinary old living room floor. Round and round the oval track it went, the brave little engine proudly pulling a string of cars—box car with doors that slid open and closed, cattle car with cattle inside and a loading platform by the track, tanker with a neat, curved ladder, gondola with an actual load of coal, and a dark red caboose. The girls were *oohing* and *ahhing* over dolls and roller skates. Maisie had a tricycle. But I had eyes only for my train. Afraid to show my delight lest the expression of it fall short of its source, I stationed myself at the transformer, and in a business-like manner acted as though I were an old veteran of electric trains, but the fine detail of the engine and the brightness of its headlight stirred my heart. I dropped a tablet down the smoke stack and turned up the speed, and then lay down on my stomach to enjoy at eye level the way it came around a bend in the track, puffing smoke. The room was filled with the smell that comes only from a new electric train, and my joy was complete.

Daddy, meanwhile, was starting a fire in the coal grate. When he had it going, we all went out into the cold, dark front yard to shoot fireworks. I didn't mind leaving my train for a while. It would be there when I went back in, and that knowledge had changed my world. I had everything I wanted.

Because the childless neighbors were still asleep, we could not light firecrackers, but there was no prohibition against sparklers. While Mammy held Johnny in her arms, the girls and I were twirling burning brands, fire-writing in the darkness, inhaling sparkler smoke, and shrieking at the tiny bites of dying flakes of ash on our hands. Then we all stood back while Daddy shot Roman candles. I wanted to do one too, but Daddy said no, I was still too young. I didn't really mind. Inside was my Lionel. The soft whush and pomp of each colored ball of fire and its brilliant arc in the darkness was a celebration of the train.

The night gave way to gray first light. The fireworks were gone. We went back in to still unexamined gifts—for me a box of Lincoln Logs. I dumped them onto the floor and went to work building a bridge over the track.

Sister and I wanted to call our friends, but Mammy said we would have to wait until after breakfast; no one else in town got up as early as we did on Christmas morning.

"Oh yeah?" I said. "Phil does."

In miraculous confirmation the phone rang and sure enough, that's who it was. "What'd you get?" he blurted. "I got an electric train."

My spirits sank. Having to say, "I did too" to Phil was a bitter pill to swallow. "What kind is yours?"

"A Lionel steam engine and freight train with real cows in the cattle car."

"Mine's a diesel," he said. "Steam engines are old-timey."

"They are not."

"They are too."

So it went with Phil and me, every statement a challenge, every answer an opportunity to go one up. I invited him to my house after breakfast and we would play with my train, but he couldn't, he said. They were getting ready to go to Georgia to see his grandmother.

We too were going to our grandmother's, just up the street, but I did not want to leave my train for that long. What I wanted was to show it off. I called Bobby, but he said he had gotten a train too, and I could come see his if I wanted to. Since he lived across the street from Mama and we were going in that direction anyway, his suggestion made sense. After breakfast I rode my bike up to his house.

With three sisters Bobby was more badly outnumbered than I was, and his living room was frothy with girl stuff. But in the midst of their dolls and tea sets lay his train, circling the track. It was the centerpiece of the family's Christmas. I examined it carefully. It was a steam engine

47

like mine but his box car doors didn't open and close and he didn't even have a cattle car. The difference gave me pleasure, but I could see no difference between Bobby's happiness and my own.

✿

There was nothing to do at Mama's, nothing to play with while I waited for dinner. The girls had their dolls, but I had only my pocket knife. I went out back to find a stick to whittle.

Mama's backyard was broken into small bowers enclosed by shrubs and garden borders, which gave it the feeling of a house with several rooms. I found a stick and settled on a slab of granite in one of the little gardens. It was chilly and firecrackers were going off all over our side of town, but for some reason it didn't feel much like Christmas. I don't know how long it took for me to realize that a sound I'd been hearing for a while—a regular, muffled *thonk*—was not the repercussion of distant fireworks, as I had supposed, but something much nearer. The sounds were coming from the back of the yard, in the vicinity of the old stable. I went to investigate, and there was Howard, chopping wood. What in the world was he doing working on Christmas Day? He was wearing the same old tattered army jacket that he'd had on last night. He must have slept in the stable. I didn't announce myself but stole closer. There was no one else around, yet he was engaged in conversation, swinging an ax and jabbering on in that rapid, husky whisper.

"You just stand up there now and don't fall down. I gots to chop you, what I gots to do. Chop you right now." *Thonk!* "Keep Mama warm tonight, what you gon' do. Keep Mama warm." *Thonk!*

I approached. He started when he saw me, though I had not meant to surprise him. He smiled. "What you doing, Jimmy, slipping up on me in the cold?"

"Nothing."

I supposed that Howard knew that this was Christmas Day—hadn't he come up to Mama's door last night and said, "Christmas gif'?" But what he conceived Christmas to be I could not imagine. I wanted to tell him about my train—I could think of nothing else to talk about—but Howard had no idea of what an electric train might be. Or of Santa Claus either, for that matter. It dawned on me that he had never waked up on Christmas morning to find presents under a tree. Had never lived in a house even that had a Christmas tree. In any case, he was spending his Christmas day chopping firewood for Mama. I turned away and headed back to the house.

The kitchen was warm and full of women—Aunt Mae and Aunt Sis, Mammy, and, presiding over the commotion, Mama. I told her that Howard was out back chopping wood.

"Oh he is? Well, run get him, son. Tell him I have something for him."

I hurried back out. The little man who wanted nothing but needed everything was about to receive a Christmas present. I was eager to see what.

He was still holding conversation with the wood when I found him. "Howard, Mama wants you. She has something for you."

He stopped and wiped his nose on his sleeve but to my surprise made no move to return with me to the house. I hung around for a minute or two then dawdled on back.

In the crowded kitchen I was underfoot, but I didn't want to miss whatever Mama meant to give him. I found a corner and laid low. Before long there was a tap at the door. Aunt Mae opened it. "Howard. You'll just have to come back later. We're busy with dinner right now."

Mae did not mean to be unkind. There was no ugliness in her tone. But she was brisk and business-like.

"I sent for him," Mama said. Mae yielded the floor to her mother and returned to the congealed salad she was preparing.

"I'll be right back," Mama told Howard, then closed the door against the cold. She left the kitchen but returned in a minute, stepped out onto the back porch, and closed the door again. I had seen no present in her hand. She must have gone to get money to pay him for chopping the wood, nothing more than that, a half dollar or so that he had coming anyway. I wandered up to the living room. Daddy and Uncle Bob were talking. I found a book and stretched out on the floor.

Firecrackers had been so constant in the neighborhood that I had long since ceased hearing them, but an unusually loud report—a cherry bomb, it sounded like—caused Bob to jump. Covering his ears with his hands he leaned forward, then shook his head vehemently, as though to rid it of something inside his skull. "I can't stand it," he said, then stood up and left the room.

I looked at Daddy, not sure that my uncle's trouble was something I had any business asking about, but Daddy saw the question in my face. "The firecrackers remind Bob of the war," he said.

My earliest experience of my Uncle Bob—a story I'd been told more than once—occurred not long before he was shipped out to Australia. I was not yet a year old. He was a young lieutenant home on leave. Having discovered that I needed changing, he was bent over me, trying to

51

figure out the folds of the diaper, and I cut loose. Bob avoided a wet uniform, he told my parents, by "hosing it aside, onto the floor." A couple of days before he was to leave for Australia, Mama and Pop drove Sis down to Alabama, and she and Bob were married in the chapel at Fort McClellan. The next day he left for Australia and did not return home until the fall of 1945. It was in that very living room that Mama would show me on the globe Australia and the Phillippines. From Australia Bob sent home a cigarette box with a picture of a kangaroo on the top. I would play with it while Mama read me Bob's letter about the baby kangaroo—he called it a joey—his company adopted as a pet. I hoped desperately that he would bring it home.

I remembered right after his return playing on the rug with his uniform insignia, his campaign ribbons, his captain's bars, the crossed rifles of the infantry, the Bronze Star. During the years since then he had completed law school and recently returned to Darlington to open a practice. Six years younger than Daddy, he had a full head of hair, and even then I knew he was cool. He was my hero. But he couldn't handle firecrackers.

"Why doesn't Mama give Howard a Christmas present?" I asked Daddy.

"Well, son," he said, "Mama does a lot for Howard all year around."

Bob returned to the room. "You can't give Howard anything," he said. "He won't even take a hand-me-down coat. But don't you worry about Howard. Howard has more money than your Daddy and me put together."

That statement was so obviously absurd that I assumed Bob was teasing me.

"Bob's right," Daddy said. "Every time he makes a dime he brings it to Mama to put in the bank for him, and he never spends a thing."

"But Mama just now paid him for chopping wood."

"She wasn't paying him, son. She was giving him his last bank statement. That shows how much money he has in the bank. She manages his account for him, and once a month when his statement comes, she gives it to him. He'd rather have that than anything else in the world."

When one is eight Christmas dinner can be more of an ordeal than a feast. Daddy asked Bob to carve the turkey, his prerogative as older son, because, he said, Bob was

53

better at it than he was. Mae corrected our table manners until Daddy told her to leave us alone. Both he and Bob called her "Daughter," as their father had, and for the same reason Daddy called Bob "Son." It must have sounded confusing to an outsider, but we always understood who was addressing whom.

"Which fork do I use for my salad, Daughter?" Bob asked Mae. "I never can remember."

Mae deflected the gibe with a smile. I think she actually enjoyed being teased by her brothers. "Is that how it's done at Converse?" one or the other would ask, and she would look at the rest of us with a smile. "Aren't they silly?" she would say.

Dessert was always fruit cake and ambrosia, a choice made with the grownups rather than children in mind, but we were not allowed to leave the table until dinner was over. Once the table was cleared, the long wait would begin again with an afternoon in which there was nothing to do.

No point in going over to Bobby's. Like Phil's family, they had left to visit a grandmother. Daddy and Uncle Bob stretched out on sofas and went to sleep. Knowing better than to whine about being bored, I told Mammy that I was going back down to our house to play with my train.

※

Most of the houses on our block of Sanders Street were occupied, as I have said, by widows and elderly couples. As I rode my bicycle down the broken sidewalk, its cracked squares uplifted by the roots of oak trees, I met no children at play with brand new toys, heard no laughter, no sounds of joy, but only the desultory pop and crackle of distant fireworks. The houses sat in bland repose, as they always did, indifferent to celebration. The afternoon had turned cloudy.

Our front door opened directly onto the living room. Inside it was almost dark and somehow it seemed chillier than outside. I turned on the overhead light. The floor was strewn with the wreckage of Santa Claus: torn wrapping paper, discarded boxes, limp stockings and the apples and oranges that had filled them, and the room smelled of dead ashes. I stepped on a pecan and it cracked beneath my heel. This was the work of my parents, Daddy spending more money than he could afford that we might have all this stuff. The luster of each present, even the train, was diminished by my knowledge that it had until a few days ago sat on a store shelf. I pictured my parents making the purchases. The Lionel was not the one I had seen in the window, but I remembered the price tag.

I plugged in the transformer and listened to it hum. Turned the switch and the train jumped into action. It circled the track, again and again, but playing with it by myself was not as much fun as I had thought it would be.

I lay down on my stomach, my chin propped up by my hands, and watched the train go round. The next thing I knew I was being jostled awake. Daddy was on his knees beside me. "You ought to turn off your train before you go to sleep," he said.

"I didn't mean to," I said.

I got up and sat on the sofa, but Daddy remained on the floor. "I bet we could make a good tunnel out of one of these boxes," he said. "Run get a knife."

I produced my Boy Scout knife, proud to be so handy, and watched closely. Daddy was good at making simple things to play with: a shoe box with windows and a flashlight inside had become a trolley car for me to drag up and down the sidewalk at night; a spool, a rubber band, a piece of crayon, and a pencil became a self-propelled tractor, at least a dozen of which had been confiscated by my teachers.

Daddy was sawing out doors in a cardboard box. When the tunnel was finished, he placed the box astride the track and drove the engine into it. "Now turn off the light," he said. When I did, the tunnel glowed from the engine's headlamp.

"How's that?" he asked.

I got down from the sofa and stretched out, eye to eye with the engine in the tunnel. "Fine," I said.

Daddy had known that day, of course, that I knew the truth about Santa Claus, but he didn't tell me that Mammy had called the president of Lionel to make sure I would get the train for Christmas. Maybe for his own sake he wanted to hold on to the pretense just a while longer that I was still a little boy. In any case, he left it for her to tell me fifty years later. In doing so, she gave me the train again, the train and that Christmas and Daddy playing with me on the floor, and also Howard. Not that she mentioned him—he didn't even cross her mind, I'm sure—but once she prompted my heart to remember he showed up.

When Aunt Mae saw him that night, she said, "Howard, what do you mean coming here?" I don't know the answer to that question now anymore than Mae did the night she asked it; I know only that I heard a tapping on the door and opened it and there he was.

The Pageant

The Pageant

※

hey came rolling into our yard one Saturday afternoon in an old piece of a car that turned out upon inspection to have once been a Ford. I was sitting on the front steps. According to the battered licence plates, they had driven the car from Michigan, though how long the trip had taken the plates didn't say. A man and a woman piled out.

It would be another year before Elvis Presley burst upon the scene, but when he did, he reminded me of the man who drove up to our house that day—greased black hair combed in what used to be called a waterfall and thick sideburns. The woman was too plain to remind me of anyone. She placed her hands at the small of her back and stretched, working out the kinks. They had seen our ad in the paper—

apartment for rent, furnished. They approached the porch, the man walking with the severe limp of a polio survivor. I greeted them and called for my mother.

We had recently moved from the little brown-shingled house on Sanders Street to a large, two-story Victorian on the other side of town. With more room than the family needed, my parents had decided to rent out one side of the upstairs, but they had not expected a blue collar Yankee who drove a pieced together wreck of a car. Where would he park it? Not in front of the house. My mother took the couple upstairs and showed them the apartment. They found it satisfactory but thought the rent too high. They wanted to look around some more.

When my mother presented the situation to my father at supper that night, he said they probably wouldn't come back.

"But what if they do?" Mammy said. "I'm the one who will have to deal with them."

"We're under no obligation to take those people, Caroline. They're not from around here, and you don't know the first thing about them—how long they plan to stay, what kind of work he does, nothing. They could be on the run for all we know."

"I know, but the woman told me she thinks she might be expecting. I don't see how we can just close the door in their faces."

My mother knew what that felt like. In January of 1945, just a couple of weeks after the Christmas Eve trip from Norfolk, Daddy was sent to a base in New Jersey. Expecting to go to sea at any time, he wanted us with him. Upon our arrival, it was Mammy's job to find an apartment. She had told us many times since of how she went from house to house in the snow, carrying a baby in her arms and dragging a whining three-year-old, only to have door after door slammed in her face.

"Well, I s'pect you're worrying about nothing,," Daddy said. "From what you say, it doesn't sound like they'll be back."

But they were, that same night. Their names were Duane and Joyce.

Among the changes in my life that year, strangers under our roof seemed one of the less significant. In June I had become a certified teenager, in September an eighth grader—in those days a no-man's land between grammar school and high school. We had moved in October, bought our first television, and recently my voice had started to betray me. At the most inopportune times, the deeper pitch that had lately developed would crack without warning into a falsetto higher than the voice of a girl. I would grow conscious of the zits on my face and blush. In fact, I blushed so easily and so brightly that classmates made a game of embarrassing me just to watch me light up. Every move I made, it seemed, turned to disaster. When the youth director at our church asked me to be the narrator for the Christmas pageant, I told my parents that I didn't want to do it.

"Why not?" Mammy asked.

"You have to memorize all those Bible verses. It's just like school."

"You've never had any trouble memorizing things."

"Nobody else is going to be in it."

Most of my friends were Baptist or Presbyterian. The few Methodists in my class—Steve, Bill, and the two Marys—had already grown too cool for folk dancing in the fellowship hall and dropped out of Methodist Youth Fellowship. But cool didn't matter to my parents. "When you are a member of an organization," Mammy explained, "you participate in its activities."

"I don't even want to be in MYF," I squawked. "That was y'all's idea in the first place, and it's not fair to make me be in the Christmas pageant."

"We're not going to make you, son. That is your decision. But if you decide against it, you're going to have to come up with a better reason than just not wanting to. What would you tell Eleanor?"

Eleanor was the youth director, a full-time staff member just out of college, where she must have majored in planning meaningful programs for young people. I liked her well enough, but she seemed little different from the women who ran my life at school all week.

My real reasons for not wanting the part were as confusing as everything else in my life. On the one hand, I was so painfully self-conscious that I could not bring myself to stand before the public, but on the other I hungered to be noticed. I resolved the conflict by convincing myself that there was no glory in narrating a Christmas play for little children. But if I could not explain those things to my mother, I certainly couldn't explain them to Eleanor. The only person who would understand was Joyce upstairs.

We had become friends in a hurry. My room was across the hall from their apartment. One night not long after they moved in, Joyce knocked at my door and asked if I would like to come over for a piece of cake. I had a vague, uneasy feeling that my parents would not approve of the visit, especially since Duane was not at home, but I went anyway.

Joyce was nineteen, five years younger than her husband. They had started dating when she was not much older than I was. Two years later she dropped out of school to marry him. She was sorry now that she hadn't waited, but Duane was a hard man to put off, she said.

She asked if I had a girlfriend.

I blushed, wave upon wave of heat, until I thought my face might break into flame. There was nothing I wanted more than a girlfriend. Every other boy in the eighth grade, it seemed, had one. A girlfriend was the ticket of legitimacy as a teenager. But I had had no success in attracting female attention. How could I expect to? My crewcut hair was straight and mousey brown; my mouth was full of wire; and my body was still the body of a child. I had tried out for junior varsity football, mainly because I thought my father expected me to, and failed to make the team. I didn't even have good grades. There were times when I hated myself.

My crimson face was answer enough for Joyce. She might have said what most adults would have said—"Oh you have plenty of time yet for girls" or "Girls are nothing but a lot of trouble"—but she didn't. What she said, with a fiercely partisan look on my behalf, was, "I don't know what's wrong with the girls in your school, but they don't know what they're missing."

The fact that she was wrong about that didn't matter. What did was her sincerity. She meant it. I was too embarrassed to continue the conversation. I mumbled thanks and left.

❧

A girl in our class named Suzanne had invited our crowd to a hayride. In spite of not having a girlfriend I was looking forward to it. Her father was going to fill a wagon with hay, hitch it up to a tractor, and pull us around the dirt roads of his farm. Boys and girls together. Who could tell what might happen? I had my eye on Betsy. If she would sit with me, that would mean we were going togther—a public statement, like initials carved in the trunk of a tree.

The night was clear and nippy, and a big yellow harvest moon rose above the pines. We were all bundled up, and the girls, at their mothers' insistence, had brought blankets. While we waited on the porch for the wagon to come around, the boys gathered at one end in a tight, protective circle, jostling and teasing and giggling, but when the tractor pulled up and we began climbing in, boys and girls paired off as though the pairings had been pre-arranged. Where had they learned how to do that? I looked for Betsy in the dark, stumbling about in the deep hay. There she was, already snuggled up by that new boy with the dark wavy hair. Did he have his arm around her? He had no right. Betsy and I had known each other since kindergarten; our parents knew each other. I looked for Mary, but she was with her ninth-grade football player, and Steve had claimed pretty Peggy. It was a game of musical chairs, and I was the one left standing.

It is easy at this distance to laugh at the follies of adolescence—the overheated hormones, the enlarged ego, the unrelenting self-consciousness. But if I brought into adulthood any scars from youth, the wounds occurred the night of that damned hayride, that and the many other similar nights I inflicted upon myself that year.

Joyce eased the pain, though not by addressing my troubles. She did it by offering her friendship, by not letting me take myself as seriously as I was inclined to, by treating me as an adult. I learned to drink coffee at Joyce's kitchen table, and it was from Joyce that I first heard the word pregnant actually used by a woman in that condition.

"I lost my first one," she told me one day.

She was standing at the stove, pouring boiling water into cups of instant coffee. Unable to see her face, I didn't know if she meant that she had had a miscarriage or if the baby had been born dead or if it had died later. I didn't know what to say.

"And the funny part of it is, that was the one that me and Duane had to get married over."

Was that what she had meant when she'd said that Duane was a hard man to put off?

She brought the coffee to the table, set down a cup for me. "That's real hot now."

"When is this one coming?" I asked.

"Oh," she said, "not before summer."

"Will y'all still be here then?"

Joyce pushed a strand of hair out of her face and tucked it behind an ear. "Duane don't like to stay in one place too long. We've been married going on three years and I've done lost track of how many places we've lived at."

Duane had told us when they moved in that he was a short-order cook looking for work, but he had other skills too if he couldn't find a job flipping hamburgers. We had been wondering now for a couple of weeks what he was up to. We had heard nothing of a job, yet he was gone most of the day and often at night. I decided that I knew Joyce well enough by now to ask where he went, not from idle curiosity but in the hope that they would remain in Darlington at least until their baby came. "Where does Duane go all the time?" I asked.

"To the poolroom."

The poolroom?

"That's what he does for a living, I reckon you'd say, but it's not a good way to live, not with a family. I just wish we could find us a place and light for a while. If Duane could get him a real job, we could rent us a little house of our own. But I can't say nothing to him about it. Duane can be real sweet when he wants to, but that's one subject he's not too sweet about."

"Why do y'all have to keep moving?"

"Sometimes we don't have no choice."

"Why not?"

"You ask too many questions, Jimmy. I probably shouldn't have said that much."

"Has Duane been in trouble?"

In a tone of mock exasperation Joyce said, "Jimmy?" and reached over and tweaked my nose. "Don't you know that curiosity killed the cat? But no, not with the law, if that's what you're worried about."

"I'm not worried. I just don't want y'all to leave."

My mother called up the stairs, as she usually did if she thought I might be across the hall. When I was, she would have a chore for me. This time she wanted to know if I had told Eleanor what I was going to do about the pageant.

"You're going to have to tell her something by tomorrow. It's not fair to keep her waiting like this."

I groaned. I knew that in the end I would do it. I felt that I had no choice. But I resented the pressure and was in no mood to cooperate cheerfully. That night I complained about the situation to Joyce.

"Oh," she said, "we used to have Christmas pageants at our church back home. They were so much fun. Me and my sister Cheryl were always angels. All the girls were except the one that got to be Mary."

The possibility that Joyce had come from a background that included church and family had never occurred to me. If so, wouldn't she be wanting to go home for Christmas?

"In that old car?" she said.

"You could go on the bus or something."

"And whose going to buy the tickets? Santa Claus? Duane wouldn't go anyway, even if we did have the money. Are you going to tell that lady you will?"

"I guess so."

"As long as you're going to do it, Jimmy, you might as well make up your mind to enjoy it."

"How can you enjoy something that's not any fun to start with?"

"Well, let's see. You could pretend that the people in the audience had all come from a foreign country that had never heard about Jesus, and you were the one that got picked to tell them. That might be kind of fun, don't you think?"

"I don't know. I guess."

In the few weeks that Duane and Joyce had lived in the apartment, they had not gone to church as far as I knew, nor had I heard Joyce talk about Jesus. For that reason her suggestion somehow removed the Bible story from the boring context of church and religion and made it seem real, or at least of real importance.

"I'll make you a deal," Joyce said. "If you promise me to do your very best in the pageant, I'll promise you that I'll come to see you in it."

"Really?"

"Really."

At Sunday School the next morning, right out of nowhere, a pretty girl walked into the room. Her hair was thick and honey-colored and she wore a red corduroy dress over stiff crinolines. Her name was Sheila, she said; her family had recently moved to town and were planning to join our church. She was in the seventh grade, which explained why I had not seen her at school. When I saw Eleanor between Sunday School and church, I told her I'd be glad to be the narrator for the pageant. I figured Sheila would be impressed by the importance of my role.

At the first practice I learned that Sheila was going to be an angel, though not just any angel; she would be the one who announces to the stunned shepherds that unto you is born this day in the city of David a Savior who is Christ the Lord. As narrator, I would introduce her.

I had no trouble memorizing my lines. At the next practice I delivered them perfectly, but if Sheila was impressed, she showed no sign of it. She smiled when I spoke to her, but she smiled the same way at everyone. How was I to break the ice? I would ask Joyce. Meanwhile, I'd just go on being as cool as I knew how.

✣

The pageant was scheduled for Sunday night before Christmas. On the Monday night before that, as I was going up the stairs to my room, Joyce stepped out into the hall. Something was wrong. I could tell by the way she was holding herself, by her pale face beneath the bare light bulb that hung from a drop cord. "Get your mother," she said. "Please hurry."

I yelled for Mammy before I was halfway down, and she was on her way up before I reached the bottom. "Stay here," she ordered as she went by. In less than three minutes she was back. "Call the poolroom," she said, "and tell Duane to get himself home right now. Tell him Joyce needs a doctor. I'm going back upstairs."

Daddy was out that night, we were not sure where, and we had no other car. I looked up the number of the Blue Goose and dialed it. An irritated voice answered.

"Is Duane there?"

"Who? I can't hear you."

"Duane."

"Duane who?"

I told him.

"Who wants to know?"

"His wife."

"I bet she does."

"Listen, this is an emergency."

"It always is."

The owner and operator of the poolroom was a friend of my father's. I knew him as a customer at Daddy's filling station. "If you don't let me talk to Duane"—my voice broke on the name, but I forged on—"I'm going to tell Doug."

"Who is this?"

"Just let me talk to Duane, please."

"Get lost, punk."

I could think of only one thing to do. I grabbed my jacket from the coat rack in the hall. My sisters asked me what was going on. "Tell Mammy I've gone to get Duane," I said, feeling heroic.

It was cold and misty outside. Down the back steps, I broke into a sprint, crossed the backyard, and though it was pitch dark I hit the opening in the hedge row without slowing up, cleared a low hogwire fence into a weedy field, and raced past the Law's house out onto Cashua Street. My way was clear now—two blocks of open sidewalk to the square. Before me shone the courthouse, festooned with colored lights. I was in high gear. For Joyce's sake. Into the square I sprinted and around the southeast corner, the wet sidewalk a blur of reflected color, the lighted store windows a blur as I sped past. Into South Main and there was the poolroom, the goose on the sign outlined in neon blue. I slowed to a breathless walk, thought of Joyce, and boldly opened the forbidden door. People stopped their play and looked at me.

Cones of dusty light illumined the green felt tables. A smell of chalk and talcum overlay the mingled odors of cigarettes and beer. Through layers of blue smoke I looked for Duane, but I didn't see him. The young man behind the counter, the smartaleck I had talked to on the phone, asked me what I wanted, but before I could answer, Duane was limping toward me. "Are you looking for me, Jimmy?"

"Joyce needs you," I gasped, still out of breath.

"What's wrong?"

"I don't know. My mother said she needs a doctor."

Duane began unscrewing the two parts of his cue stick, placed them in a black case, and said, "Let's go, sport."

I felt like the boy in *Shane* when the famous gunfighter acknowledges him in the saloon.

As Duane and I walked toward the back door, play resumed, the knocking and soft tocking of balls. Somebody called out, "Old lady sent for you, slick?"

Duane's car sounded like an airplane taking off. He spun it about, throwing gravel, and squealed his tires as he swung into Main Street. "You ran all the way up here to get me? Why didn't you call?"

"I did. They wouldn't let me speak to you."

Duane swore.

There was always a police car at the corner of the square and Pearl Street. I mentioned that to Duane as he roared into the square.

"I hope they try," he said.

Somehow we made it, skidding to a stop on the wet pavement in front of the house. Without waiting for me, Duane bolted from the car, bounded up the walk and through the front door. It took me a moment in the dark to discover that the door on my side lacked a handle. I slid across the sprung seat, beneath the steering wheel, and climbed out. By the time I got inside, Duane was upstairs. I started up, but Sister stopped me. "Mammy said for you to stay down here." She enjoyed sounding bossy.

I felt that my special friendship with Joyce, not to mention my heroic run, entitled me. I ignored my sister.

"You better not, Jimmy. Mammy was serious and you're going to be in big trouble. It's about the baby. She called Doctor Mac and he's coming."

Doctor Mac Wilcox had delivered three of the four of us, Maisie at home because she came so fast. He had set my broken foot, stitched up my cuts, and given us dozens of shots, mostly in his office but sometimes at our house in the middle of the night when a sick child awoke gasping for breath or crying with an earache or hot with fever. I had always associated him with needles, but back in the summer, when I was taken to his office for a hernia complaint, Doctor Mac had opened a drawer and shown me a wealth of arrowheads. Then invited me to choose two for myself.

"I guess I'd better wait for him," I told my sister, "so I can show him where to go."

I didn't have to wait long. When I heard the knock , I let the doctor in and pointed him upstairs. Before long, Mammy came down; she said Joyce was going to be all right, but that was all she said. She was busy making a pot of coffee. Doctor Mac came down sooner than I had expected. He declined coffee and took Mammy out into the hall. I poured a cup for myself.

Joyce had almost lost the baby, he told her; she might yet. She would have to take it easy and get plenty of bed rest. And she could not be going up and down our long flight of stairs. First thing tomorrow morning, Duane was going to start looking for a ground floor apartment.

I didn't see Joyce again until the day they moved. Duane had found a duplex over by the Dixie Cup plant. He brought her down the steps in his arms, limping heavily, with her laughing and protesting all the way. At the foot of the steps he put her down. She looked at me. "Duane told me how you ran to get him the other night, all the way to the pool room. That was really sweet." She gave me a warm hug. All I could feel were breasts. "You folks are going to have to come see us now when we get settled in," she said. Duane was impatient to get going. "You know where it is?"

Mammy said she did.

"I'll see you Sunday night, Jimmy."

At the Christmas pageant. With all her trouble she had not forgotten her promise.

The pageant took place in the sanctuary. The pulpit had been removed so that the area might serve as a stage. Where the pulpit had been, stood a three-sided shed and within the shed a bale of hay and a cradle. I led the choir out of the choir room, made my way through the choir loft and came to a lectern placed to the right of the shed. On the lectern sat a Bible and a flashlight, aids to be used should I forget my lines. Hidden in shadow I was to be a voice. To tell a pagan audience the story of Jesus, Joyce had suggested. She was somewhere out there in the dark. Maybe Duane too, though I doubted it. As the choir sang, "Oh Come All Ye Faithful," I looked out over the audience, but the sanctuary was too dark for me to spot even my parents. The magnificent stained glass windows, depicting events in the life of Jesus, glowed with vivid color, backlighted by the streetlights outside.

I reminded myself that I had no reason to be nervous. I knew my passages backward and forward. I had said them aloud dozens of times in the past week. On the last words of the hymn I cleared my throat.

> *The people that walked in darkness have seen a great*
> *light: they that dwell in the land of the shadow of*
> *death, upon them hath the light shined.*
> *For unto us a child is born, unto us a son is given;*
> *and the government shall be upon his shoulder; and*
> *his name shall be called Wonderful, Counsellor, the*
> *mighty God, the everlasting Father, the Prince of Peace.*

After "Joy to the World" I spoke again.

*And it came to pass in those days, that there went
out a decree from Caesar Augustus, that all the world
should be taxed. (And this taxing was first made when
Cyrenius was governor of Syria.) And all went to be
taxed, everyone into his own city, and Joseph also
went up from Galilee, out of the city of Nazereth,
into Judea, into the city of David, which is called
Bethlehem; (because he was of the house and lineage
of David;) to be taxed with Mary his espoused wife
being great with child.*

The door of the vestibule in the rear of the sanctuary
opened and here came Mary and Joseph. There was no
donkey for her to ride nor even a semblance of her being
great with child, but they proceeded slowly down the aisle as
though she were, seventh graders, he in a bathrobe, she
draped in shades of blue, and she was taller than her husband.
They came up into the light that shone upon the shed. She
sat down on the bale of hay, and Joseph stood behind her.

*And so it was that while they were there, the days
were accomplished that she should be delivered. And
she brought forth her firstborn son and wrapped him in
swaddling clothes and laid him in a manger; because
there was no room for them in the inn.*

Mary reached into the cradle and brought out a doll and held it lovingly in her arms.

And there were in the same country shepherds abiding
in the field, keeping watch over their flock by night.

I waited for the door at the rear of the sanctuary to open, and here they came: a file of little Methodist boys wearing taped-on beards and drab bathrobes and carrying their shepherds' crooks, just as I had several years before. When they had almost reached the altar rail, I resumed the recitation.

And lo the angel of the Lord came upon them . . .

A light was switched on and there to my right, elevated on a box, stood the beautiful Sheila. Glitter sparkled on her white angel costume.

And the glory of the Lord shone round about them
and they were sore afraid. And the angel said unto them . . .

With a voice that was still the voice of a little girl, Sheila picked up the sentence and raced without expression or inflection to the end of her part.

*Fear not for behold I bring you good tidings of great
joy which shall be to all people for unto you is born
this day in the city of David a Savior who is Christ
the Lord, and this shall be a sign unto you: you shall
find the babe wrapped in swaddling clothes and lying
in a manger.*

With that breathless conclusion she returned the narration to me.

*And suddenly there was with the angel a multitude of
the heavenly host praising God and saying Glory to
God in the highest and on earth Peace, good will toward men.*

As the choir stood to sing "Hark, the Herald Angels," a troop of little angelettes, among them my two sisters, emerged from the shadows off to the right and arranged themselves around Sheila. This was going great, I thought. I had neither stammered nor stumbled. I must have been impressing the daylights out of Sheila. And somewhere out there in the dark sat my friend Joyce. I felt so good that I delivered the next part with unusual energy and color.

*And it came to pass, as the angels were gone away
from them into heaven, the shepherds said one to*

another, Let us now go even unto Bethlehem and see
this thing that has come to pass, which the Lord
hath made known unto us. And they came with haste . . .

The little shepherds made their way around the end of
the altar rail and approached the shed.

. . . and found Mary and Joseph and the babe lying
in a manger.

I breathed an almost audible sigh of relief. The choir
sang "What Child Is This?" I had made it through the
hard part and had only the wise men to go. When the door
to the vestibule swung open, I made the switch to Matthew.

Now when Jesus was born in Bethlehem of Judea in the
days of Herod the king, behold, there came wise men
from the east—

and that's when it happened. At the word *east* my voice
broke. The sound that issued from my throat was that of a
four-year-old. My face and neck grew warm, then hot.
Thank goodness for the dark. Nothing to do but plow on.
And then someone giggled—one of the cast. It was not
loud; in fact, it sounded involuntary, as though unsuccess-

fully suppressed, but it triggered a response from the dumb little shepherds huddled at the feet of the Holy Family. Sure that it was Sheila who had started it, I could not remember to save my life what came next. I switched on the flashlight. The Bible was opened not to Matthew but to Isaiah. Where was Matthew? I flipped pages. A dislodged stone was escalating into a full scale avalanche, and I saw no way to stop it.

"Where is he that is born King of the Jews," someone whispered from the right. A girl. Was it Sheila? With a loud voice I said:

For we have seen his star in the east and are come to worship
him.

There were no more giggles, but I was terrified that my voice would betray me again. With an effort to deepen the pitch, I proclaimed:

When Herod had heard these things he was troubled
and all Jerusalem with him. And when he had gathered
all the chief priests and scribes of the people
together, he demanded of them where Christ should be born.

I stumbled on, faltering, sounding like an idiot, reciting by rote.

When they had heard the king, they departed; and lo
the star which they saw in the——

There was that word again. I gathered myself, focused my resolve, took a deep breath, and got it out, not realizing that I sounded sillier than I would have if my voice had broken again.

——the east, went before them till it came and stood
over where the young child was.

When the choir had finished "We Three Kings," the wise men in their brightly colored garb and crowns of gilt and tinsel were assembled with their gifts before the manger, and I raced for the finish line.

And when they were come into the house, they saw
the young child with Mary his mother and fell down
and worshiped him, and when they had opened their
treasures they presented unto him gifts: gold and
frankincense and myrrh.

At last. The congregation joined the choir in all verses of "Silent Night" and then the lights came on. I fled to the choir room and plopped down into a chair. Robes swirled around me as they were removed and hung up. Amid the din of conversation, a couple of people patted me on the back and said, "Good job." Friends of my parents, they were just trying to make me feel better. I had not done a good job. What had Joyce said? Pretend that I was the one who got to tell the story of Jesus to an unbelieving world? All I could think of was the inadequacy of my voice, and I was so embarrassed. I wanted to see Joyce, but I refused to go out into the sanctuary to mingle with people who would compliment me just because I happened to bump into them. I hoped she would wait.

The choir room opened directly onto the outside. I went out onto the empty sidewalk to wait for my family. Christmas lights were strung from the corner where I stood all the way up Pearl to the square. Mammy and Daddy were having to wait for Sister and Maisie, and I was getting cold. Joyce hadn't come. I knew she hadn't. She would have found me by now. Duane had probably refused to drive her, but still, she had promised.

The doors of the church opened and here came my family. Approaching me, my mother said, "Where in the world have you been? We've been looking everywhere.

There were several people who wanted to speak to you, but I'm sure they've gone by now."

"Y'all didn't see Duane and Joyce, did you?"

"Duane and Joyce?" My mother seemed surprised by the question.

"She said she might come."

"Well, son, you know she has to be careful. It probably wasn't a good idea for her to get out on a night like this, but I'm sure she wanted to. I bet she was there in spirit."

I never heard from Joyce again. They might have stayed in Darlington until the boys in the pool room figured out that there was no percentage in playing Duane, or they might have left town when they moved from our house. I hoped they were still here. Joyce should not have been back on the road in her condition, especially at Christmas time. But I was never to know.

Johnny was six and knew the truth. For the first time there was no one in the family who still believed in Santa Claus. So Christmas came to the Kilgo home that year without being greeted by the quivering anticipation that had once filled the house. The most exciting gift was Johnny's red bicycle.

In recent years we had been driving to Greenwood on Christmas afternoon to spend a few days with our Lawton grandparents, but that year my grandfather Doc was too sick for company. So we stayed in Darlington and had Christmas dinner at Mama's house with Mama and Aunt Mae and Uncle Bob and Aunt Sis, who now had two little ones of their own. After dinner, Daddy asked if I wanted to go quail hunting with him and the Brown brothers that afternoon. Usually, I would have jumped at the chance, but this time I declined. I went to a movie instead.

That may be the worst way I can think of to spend Christmas afternoon if you're by yourself. When the movie was over, I walked out into a drizzly dusk and turned toward home, following the same route I had taken to the pool room just a few days before. As I approached the house, I saw that the windows were dark. Mammy and the others had not come home from Mama's as I had expected. Johnny had left his bicycle on the porch. I had to move it out of the way to get inside.

I turned on the lamp in the living room and without removing my jacket slumped down in a chair. The room was littered as it always was on Christmas afternoon with the spoils of Santa Claus—an easel with a pad of drawing paper for me, a record player, Maisie's skates, a sweater still in its box, and the inevitable apples and oranges.

Might as well plug in the tree, I thought. I got down on my hands and knees and crawled around a table, plugged in the cord, and the tree lit up. I backed out. Getting to my feet, I bumped the table, causing a clatter and a crash. Oh Lord. What had I broken? What costly present or irreplaceable vase?

It was only the manger scene, thank goodness. Figures lay in pieces on the floor, but the set had not been expensive. We had only had it for a couple of years. We could easily get another. I knelt to gather up the fragments—heads and arms of wise men and shepherds and maybe some of Joseph too. Mary was chipped but otherwise intact, and the little manger with the baby had lost a leg. I placed the pieces on the table and tried to put them back together, fitting arms to shoulders, setting heads in place, and confusing wise men with shepherds. It wasn't working. Maybe I could glue them. I arranged the fragments in the conventional choreography, sorting out the figures according to their stations, setting the chipped Virgin next to the three-legged manger, and as I did the words I had memorized came unbidden to my mind:

And the days were accomplished that she should be delivered.

*And the shepherds said one to another, let us now
go even unto Bethlehem to see this thing that has
come to pass.*

*And the star which they saw in the east went before
them till it came and stood over where the young child was.*

For the first time in my life I realized what beautiful words they were, and by that beauty they had the power to evoke the events they spoke of. I gathered up the broken pieces and cupped them in my hands. I didn't know whether I believed the story or not, but I wanted it to be true more than I had ever wanted anything.

The Hand-Carved Crèche

The Hand-Carved Crèche

✣

$\mathcal{I}$ began this Christmas letter to my granddaughter on the sixth of January, which this year was Epiphany Sunday, the day on which the church celebrates the showing of the Christ child to the wise men. January sixth is also the Twelfth Day of Christmas, traditionally the end of the holiday, when the tree is taken down and decorations put away. My efficient wife has always been in charge of that dismantling, but this year I asked her not to pack up the crèche. We are now in the last week of January and still it sits in its accustomed place on a small chest in the dining room. Looking at it gives me pleasure.

Crèches were called manger scenes when I was a child, but I don't remember that many people had them. We didn't until I was older, and that one—the one I broke—consisted of plaster figures cast from standard molds. By the time I was married, however, crèches had become popular, and that popularity produced great diversity of style, material, size, and color. In the mid-sixties when I was newly married and doing graduate work in New Orleans, I wanted one for our collection of Christmas decorations, though I didn't realize that I did until I saw the one I wanted.

It was in the window of a gift shop in the French Quarter—a crèche composed of many figures made of wood, simply carved. Jane and I both were immediately charmed. We had already learned that on those rare occasions when our tastes concurred we should buy. Unfortunately, the crèche was beyond our means. Way beyond.

"The figures are hand-carved by a family in Germany," the saleswoman explained. "We are the only outlet for this crèche in the entire United States."

"It sure is beautiful," Jane said, "but a bit too much for us, I'm afraid."

"Of course, you can buy it piecemeal," the saleswoman said. "Many people do."

Acquiring the entire set would take a good many years. In addition to the Holy Family and the three wise men, there were six shepherds and a Noah's Ark of animals— not only the obligatory sheep, cow, and donkey but camels and Arabian horses, as well as beasts of the wild, from squirrels to giraffes. "We don't plan to stay in New Orleans that long," I said.

"Oh, we ship," she said. "Anywhere in the U.S."

"How much is the Holy Family?"

"With the stable, which you would certainly need, let me see." She gave us a price. It was more than we had planned to spend on each other's presents combined.

"We'll have to think about it," Jane said.

Though we agreed on wanting the crèche, our reasons were not the same. Jane's were religious. She believed that Christmas was about the birth of Jesus, not Rudolph, Frosty, and Santa Claus, and we could acknowledge that faith by displaying a crèche in our home. My reason, on the other hand, was aesthetic. The carved wooden figures of the crèche appealed to my sensibility. To display them would show good taste.

We decided to give the Holy Family and the stable to each other for Christmas. Before we left New Orleans to spend the holidays with our families, we proudly set it out in our apartment.

Over the next several years we added to the crèche as we had planned: first, two shepherds—old men, one wearing a hat—next, the three wise men rich and colorful; next, a kneeling shepherd boy and a donkey. By the time we had collected a minimally complete manger scene we were living in Athens, Georgia, we had three children, and other great changes had taken place in our lives.

But I'm getting ahead of my story, about to leave out a character who wants to come in.

He entered my life for about four hours one day, and that was not at Christmas but in the heat of August. After he departed I never heard of him again, but here he is, at about the time Jane and I are beginning to buy the crèche.

It was the summer of 1968. We were visiting my parents, who now lived in Mama's house. Several years before, Mama had fallen and broken a hip. The fracture did not heal, and since that time she had been confined to her bed. Rather than put her in a nursing home, Mammy and Daddy sold the Victorian house on Spring Street and moved in with her. Thus the old Kilgo place, in the shadow of which I had grown up, became our home at last, though by then I was married and living somewhere else.

On the day I'm speaking of, Daddy and I were sitting in the living room arguing about the war in Vietnam while we waited for dinner. Mammy and Jane and Aunt Mae, who was coming home from Spartanburg every weekend to see her mother, were in the kitchen preparing the meal. Though Mama's house was now my parents' home and its kitchen my mother's domain, Mae seemed not to have gotten the message. Whenever she entered the front door, she became the mistress of the house again. In the kitchen now she was telling my mother, "Caroline, I think I'll let you take up the rice." Mammy rolled her eyes but went ahead and served the rice into a bowl.

Daddy and I were interrupted by the arrival of my sister Caroline, who had been out running errands. She clearly had something to tell. "Y'all listen to this," she said. "You won't believe what I just saw—a man was coming through town and he was dragging a cross."

"A cross? What kind of cross?" I asked.

"What kind do you think? The kind you crucify somebody on. Except this one has little wheels at the bottom so actually it rolls instead of drags. He's on his way to Maine."

Her excitement had brought Mammy and Jane and Mae from the kitchen.

"How do you know that?" I asked.

"He told me."

"You talked to him?" Mae asked.

"Of course, I did. He's resting right now out there beyond Bi-Lo's. He's walked all the way from Miami."

"Can we go see him?" Jane asked.

"Yeah," Caroline said. "Who else wants to?"

Not I, I thought. My sister was given to wild notions. No telling what kind of nut case this guy might be. I would hear all I wanted to know when they got back.

"I'll go," Daddy said.

We were all surprised. Daddy had no interest in what he considered weirdos.

He just thinks a man should be along, I decided.

They returned sooner than I expected. I went to the front door, and here they came up the walk—Jane, Sister, Daddy, and the man who was dragging a cross from Miami to Maine. They had actually brought him home for dinner. I was glad to see that he had left his cross out on the highway. I called Mammy and Mae from the kitchen.

The stranger was a burly man in a blue chambray shirt. His face was bronze, his eyes bright blue, and he had a great bush of sun-bleached beard. When I gripped his hand it felt like brick. In a surprisingly soft and gentle voice he said, "My name is Peter." Far from being uneasy, Peter seemed calm and self-possessed, as though he was where he was meant to be and knew it. He was honored to be invited into our home, he said, and prayed God's blessings upon the family.

"Well," Mammy said, "we're so glad to have you, Peter. Dinner will be ready in a few minutes. Jimmy will show you where to wash your hands."

When Peter returned from the bathroom, Mammy and Mae and Jane brought in the food—roast beef in gravy, rice, squash casserole, butterbeans, sliced tomatoes, hot biscuits, and sweet iced tea. Mae went back to the kitchen for something and we all took our seats. Caroline was bombarding our guest with questions. Daddy stopped her and asked Peter if he would do us the favor of a blessing.

I don't remember how the blessing went, but it was not a perfunctory table grace. It was prayer, not long but addressed to God with startling familiarity. When he had finished, the bowls began to circulate, and it occurred to me that Mae had not come back. I was about to make that observation when I realized that she was not planning to.

Peter was from Maine. He and his wife owned and operated a motel and restaurant. Or had until he heard from God. Peter was to go to Miami, God told him, and wait there for further instructions.

It seemed to me that God could have prevented a great deal of strife and anguish in Peter's marriage by breaking the news to Peter's wife at the same time. But his ways are not our ways, Isaiah reminds us. He left that task to Peter, and the results were about what you would expect. Peter set his house in order, balanced the books, and booked a flight to Miami. He promised to call when he knew more. When he did, the news was not well received. God had told him to take up his cross and walk back to Maine.

Peter's wife and his best friend, who happened to be a lawyer, took action to have Peter declared incompetent. They wanted to take the motel away from him. His wife filed for divorce. All of which grieved Peter deeply. He loved his wife and had expected to return to his former life when he got back home.

The most impressive thing about the man was not his story but, given the circumstances, the fact that he seemed to be perfectly sane. He was clearly in his right mind, poised, gracious, at peace. The more he said, the more I wanted to hear.

Caroline was full of practical questions. How did he eat? Where did he sleep? Had he been harassed by rednecks and dogs? Was the cross heavy?

His answers were just as practical. He had been fed by kind people, as we were feeding him now. He usually slept in the woods or under a bridge if it was raining. As for harassment, only once, in south Georgia, but he had welcomed that as an opportunity to tell his tormentors the story of Jesus' love. And if Caroline was interested in the weight of the cross, he invited her to try it out when we returned him to the place where he had left it.

Daddy asked in a kind way what good he thought he was doing.

Peter's blue eyes twinkled, and his voice when he answered was soft. "I have to leave that to God," he said. "My task is to be obedient. If God needs the spectacle of a man carrying a cross, the least I can do is provide it."

At some point during my college years I had waked up one morning to realize that I could no longer in good conscience say the Apostle's Creed. Whatever unexamined faith I had left home with had since been abandoned, with baseball cards and electric trains, somewhere along the way. I remained susceptible to the beauty of the Gospels, to the language of *Luke* and *John*, and to the loveliness of Jesus, but I had no use for church or any organized religion. I still felt that way as I sat at my parents' table that hot August day in 1968, yet I could not hear enough of what this pilgrim was saying. My family had never spoken so comfortably of Jesus, nor shown such unselfconscious familiarity with him. There was nothing fanatical about Peter, nothing strident in his witness, nothing religious. He made the spiritual seem altogether natural, and he did it with a grace that I found captivating.

I was embarrassed by Mae's absence from the table. With the intolerant zeal of youth I considered her a bigot and a snob. But I was wrong about that. Mae was too good to be so easily dismissed. She simply did not know how to respond to such honesty concerning God. In her world it was considered bad manners to refer to Jesus by his first name. Peter threw her off balance.

It's easy to caricature my aunt—almost impossible not to—and caricatures are seldom flattering. But the truth is that Mae loved us with all her heart and she did her best at loving God and her neighbors as herself. It was just too bad that her scruples that day would not let her break bread with our guest.

Peter spent much of the afternoon with us. When we took him back out to the highway, he shook our hands, said goodbye, and took up his cross. The last I saw of him, he was headed north on 52. A day or two later there was an article and a picture in the *Florence Morning News*, but we never heard of him again. I don't know if he made it all the way to Maine or not, or what he found if he got there. Nor do I know what he's doing in a Christmas story, unless it has to do with the effect of his witness on me.

I don't mean to say that I was converted by Peter's example, but I must confess that during that spiritually turbulent time in my life, Peter made a difference, adding authority to the witness that would ultimately prevail.

As I was saying before Peter interrupted, by the time Jane and I had collected a minimally complete crèche, our first two children were old enough to participate in setting it up. Each year we made a ritual of it. About two weeks before Christmas we would gather in the living room and open the box in which the figures had spent the last eleven months. I would place the stable on a woven mat and then read the words of Matthew and Luke, those same passages I had memorized for the pageant so many years before. At the appropriate points in the story, John and Sarah Jane would take turns removing the carved character from its tissue wrapping and put it in the right place. As Jane held baby Ann, the little group would assemble around the manger— Mary and Joseph, the three wise men, five shepherds now—one of them a girl—and assorted barnyard animals, including a chicken that perched on a post of the stable. And there the crèche would sit, Christmas after Christmas, as the children grew up and one by one left home, through holidays saddened by losses of those we loved and holidays brightened by the arrival of new little ones.

It is tempting to say that amidst the flux of all those years, the crèche has remained the same, an unchanging tradition in the Kilgo home. But that would be only partly true, for there is a sense in which the crèche has changed— it has changed in our perception of its meaning. As I take it down and put it away this year, I realize for the first time that among the gathered creatures, there are no figures of King Herod and Caesar Augustus and no High Priest. Which is a little surprising when you think about it. If God was going to keep his promise by coming to earth as a human infant, you'd think that he might have had the angels announce it to the people in charge down here, or if not to them at least to the religious authorities who had a professional interest in the event. I mean, a shimmering star and cloven skies and hosts of angel choirs would have loosened the stiffest necks. But, as I have already reminded myself, His ways are not our ways. When the time came, he chose as parents a young couple too inconsequential for anyone to pay attention to and set them on the road; he sent birth announcements to shepherds of all people— dirty, smelly, illiterate—and even worse to foreigners, who, though called wise men, must have appeared to their wives as mad as Peter the Holy Fool seemed to his.

Though it's high time the crèche were taken down and put away, I feel a surprising reluctance to begin the disman-tling. Why not leave it up all year? No law says that we have to abide by the custom of seasonal use. Jane might have another opinion, but there is a quality about the crèche that I love as much in July as I do in the dead of winter. I don't know what else to call it but coziness—the security of an enclosed space, the attraction of an *inside* seen from the *outside*. The inside needs a fire, of course, to make the windows glow with the promise of warmth. Luke's account does not mention a fire, but wouldn't you think that Joseph built one? That's the first thing you do, especially with a wife in Mary's condition. And maybe it was the glow of that fire that caught the attention of the shivering shepherds as they wandered through the dark maze of Bethlehem looking for this thing that had come to pass. The wise men were led by the star, but, still cold from the bitter desert night, they too must have enjoyed the warmth.

Their presence at the stable is false to the Biblical account, as any reader of Matthew knows—they found Jesus in a "house," apparently some weeks or even months after he was born—but the custom of crèches places them at the stable on the night the shepherds arrived. I like the symmetry of that gathering. The contrast between the two groups is extreme enough to open a space that might accommodate the rest of us. I used to do a good bit of wood carving. I still have my tools. It occurs to me that I might make a carving of Peter and his cross and set it among the other homeless guests at the manger. But I wouldn't stop with Peter; I would carve an Aunt Mae too and place her at Peter's side, and a Howard with cotton in his ears and a "What, me worry?" smile on his face, and a crippled young pool shark looking for a place for his wife to have their baby—all those broken people finding home at last in the light of the stable.

Epilogue

※

This little book had its inception in a request by our friend Madeline Van Dyck that I give a Christmas reading at the Van Dyck's annual Winter Solstice party. Unable to find anything short enough and suitable, I wrote a sketch of a childhood Christmas—the Christmas of my electric train. Little did I know that the sketch would develop into the narrative you've just read. That was suggested by Judy Long of Hill Street Press. At first, I was skeptical. The sketch was only six pages long. How was I to expand it into a book even as thin as this one? I didn't have the material. Then two ladies came to spend the Christmas holidays with us—my mother Caroline, who started telling stories, and our granddaughter Caroline, who would some day want to hear them. Together, they provided the key that unlocked stored memories.

Even so, I expected to come up with little more than nostalgic recollections of family, Santa Claus, and decorated trees. When I began to write, however, surprising things happened. In the midst of the story about the Lionel, Howard the yard man knocked on the door of my memory. While Howard was a conspicuous character during my childhood, I had no idea what he was doing in a Christmas story. Because he didn't fit the tale, I tried to leave him out, but he kept knocking, kept smiling, kept insisting. So I said, Okay, whether I understand what you're doing here or not, come on in.

After I started work on the chapter about the pageant, I spent a night at the homeless shelter sponsored by our church. I awoke at 6:00 A.M. on my pallet and found myself thinking of a young couple who rented an apartment at our house for a brief time when I was a teenager. I had not thought of them in many, many years, but in the half-conscious state of waking up, I saw them as they were, saw the car they drove, and the man's terrible limp. I could not remember their names, but what came to me was Duane and Joyce. Later, when I checked with members of my family who remembered more clearly than I, I found that I was close to being right. Again, I could not understand why they wanted to be in a Christmas story, but I honored their request as I had Howard's, and they seemed to find a place in the narrative.

By the time I came to write "The Hand-Carved Crèche," I was on the lookout for strange, improbable characters, and suddenly there was Peter, again a man unthought of for many years. Though he had come to my parents' house in August rather than December, I knew better than to try keeping him out. And only then, when I had told his story, did I discover what he and his friends were doing in my Christmas book.